EASY [illegible] LEARN

JAMIEKAN PATWA

Maizle S. Goulbourne

1st Edition

Easy Steps to Learn Jamiekan Patwa

Maizle S. Goulbourne, Kingston, Jamaica
At: maizle.jamaicanpatwa.@gmail.com
or https://fb.me/1lyRpFkUZXH8ltb

Maizle S. Goulbourne

ISBN 978-976-96608-0-9

ACKNOWLEDGEMENT

I would like to thank my loving husband, Kenneth (Welles), for his support and understanding of my long hours at nights on the computer. Also, to my children, Triguel, Nakhiah, Khristaho, Etel-Welles and Dorniqah, for their cooperation, especially when I called at odd hours to get a perspective on my thoughts.

Special thanks to my sister, Juliet, for presenting the challenge which sparked the desire within me to write this book, and for her constant support throughout, as well as helping with the editing.

FOREWORD

The publication of **Di Jamiekan Nyuu Testiment** by the Bible Society of the West Indies, generated a heightened interest in the beloved and also *much maligned* Jamaican Creole (Jamiekan Patwa). Since the publication of **Di Jamiekan Nyuu Testiment** in 2012, a number of Jamaicans and foreigners have taken a keener interest in learning this structured form of the Creole language.

This book, *Easy Steps to Learn the Jamiekan Patwa,* acts as a tutor to help both the Patwa-speaking Jamaicans and non-Patwa speakers who are interested in not just speaking the language, but also in reading and writing it. For many years, Jamiekan Patwa was mainly a spoken language, although earlier writers like Claude McKay, Una Marson, and Louise Bennett-Coverly wrote in the Jamaican dialect. However, these earlier writers used a variety of spellings, resulting in a lack of uniformity of the written word. Frederic Cassidy is rightly credited with helping to standardize the dialect, making it into the Jamaican Creole language. The Bible Society of the University of the West Indies must be commended for taking that bold step in publishing **Di Jamiekan Nyuu Testiment** in the purest form of the Jamiekan Creole, basilect. Oftentimes, I listened with great bemusement as some Jamaicans, too posh for the language of their hearts, become emotionally upset at the wonderful writers for having the temerity to publish a part of the Bible in Jamiekan Patwa.

The book, *Easy Steps to Learn the Jamiekan Patwa,* is written by Maizle S. Goulbourne, and she revealed that the spelling used is based on Frederic Cassidy's work which was modified by the Jamaican Language Unit at the University of the West Indies. In studying the lessons, I found that simultaneously reading **Di Jamiekan Nyuu Testiment** and other Patwa materials were useful in having a better understanding of the Jamiekan Creole, leading to an expansion of my Patwa vocabulary in basilect.

Undoubtedly, the reader is interested in my association with this book, so, now I will assuage your curiosity. In March 2019, I started attending a Patwa reading group in Mt Vernon, New York, and became intrigued by the enthusiasm of the non-Patwa speakers. Their inquisitiveness, especially about our many Jamaican expressions, and their restlessness to devour the language with a bolt lightning speed, compelled me to share my knowledge about the Jamiekan Patwa. I also felt a need to have a simply written guide to help grasp what I dubbed, the *new Patwa*. In a conversation with a Jamaican language arts lecturer, I related the challenges of not having a very basic beginners' book for non-Patwa speakers who were so eager to devour our native tongue. Also, for me, I desperately needed a guide to understand the structured Jamiekan Creole in order to read and write it in the basilect, the more traditional form, closely aligned with the slaves, the inventors of the language.

As a youth, the author, Maizle Goulbourne, acted in skits written in Patwa. She was also an ardent listener to the radio performances of Louise Bennet and Ranny Williams and developed a strong passion for Patwa. Maizle's desire for writing was awakened while working in the Editorial Department at the Jamaica Gleaner Company as the personal assistant to the then Editor-in-Chief. This assignment led to her becoming a regular contributor to the Sunday Gleaner.

After raising her children, Maizle went back to school at the Mico University College, and during her graduate studies, her cohort was introduced to the work of Cassidy. This was in 2008, and the translation of the Greek scriptures into **Di Jamiekan Nyuu Testiment**, was in full swing at the University of the West Indies, a mere five miles away. The group of graduate students was given excerpts in Jamaican Creole to practice and decipher the language. Despite that, the structured Jamaican Creole was challenging, and initially, they felt a bit foolish, but they battled through the assignment. In the end, they became intoxicated with delighted pride in successfully completing the Patwa task.

My first reaction was that the Patwa Bible was incomprehensible, but I was wrong! Mastering the basic concepts found in the book, *Easy Steps to Learn the Jamiekan Patwa*, made it easier to read. The book provides the reader with an uncomplicated step-by-step guide which is needed to conquer the Jamiekan Patwa. It explains the alphabetical system in great details, and the differences between the English and Patwa alphabets. The book also identifies the twelve Patwa vowels, and isolates the five single ones which are used to form the seven double vowels. Since Patwa is phonetic, the reader is coached into using these twelve vowels to recognize each vowel sound and the accompanied spellings to better understand the language.

The section on forming plurals is very useful as this is so different from standard English. To help cement the simple rules of the Patwa grammar, verb is widely covered and includes the subject verb agreement, tenses and copula with activities. To demystify the Jamiekan Patwa, the author rounded out the book with commonly used words, popular expressions, and slangs. This book will help both the Patwa speaker and non-Patwa speaker to read and write the basilectal version in a shorter time.

Juulet H. Kambl

Table of Contents

DI JAMIEKAN PATWA LANGWIJ

INTRODUCTION

The Jamiekan Patwa is a language by itself, and until recently, it was predominantly an oral language spoken mainly by Jamaicans. However, there is now a format in place which allows for the language to be read and written, making it easier to understand and more widely spoken by foreigners.

Patwa is traditionally the language of the Jamaican people, and when it is spoken by them it has a rich Jamaican flavour or lilt. In recent years, a writing system was developed to help learners understand 'How to read Jamaican' (Cassidy, cited in Di Jamiekan Nyuu Testiment, 2012).

The A-Z alphabetical system, the phonetic spelling and the short vowel sounds of the letters **a, e, i, o, u** used in this book, are based on Standard Jamaican English Language. However, Cassidy - JLU Writing System - is used to write the Patwa words. Based on this system:

- *There is no single letter* **c** *in the Patwa alphabet.* **C** is replaced with **ch**. As a result of this change, words with the *hard c* sound are spelt with **k;** and words with the *soft c* sound are spelt with an **s.**

  Examples of soft c**:** cell, decent, malice, place, vice. In Patwa, these words would become: *sel, diisent, malis, plies, vais.*

  Examples of hard c**:** accident, cake, difficult, music, vacation. In Patwa, these words would become: *aksident, kiek, difikolt, muusik, vakieshan.*

- *The letter* **Q** *does not exist* in the Patwa alphabet. However, the q-sound is found in many words. To navigate the use of q, Patwa uses the combined letters **kw.** For example, words such as: acquit, equality, equipment, liquid, question, quick, would become: akwit, *iikwaliti, ikwipment likwid, kwestiyan, kwik.*

- *The letter **U** has two distinct sounds when used in Patwa.* There is a single vowel **u**, and a double vowel **uu**. The single vowel u has a different sound from the double vowel uu.

  The single vowel **u** has a short sound, whereas the double vowel **uu** has a long sound. (To get the sound of the single vowel u, *try pronouncing the letter b or p to help you along*). Now, here are some examples.

  Single vowel **u**: book, could, good, look, should, stood, would, in English are spelt in Patwa as, *buk, kud, gud, luk, shud, stud, wud.*

  Double vowel **uu**: boot, root, food, mood, blue, glue, fruit, juice, in English are spelt in Patwa as, buut, ruut, fuud, muud, bluu, gluu, fruut, juus.

- Another letter which is not included in the Patwa alphabet is **x,** and it is substituted with letters such as, **z, gz, ks,** (as seen in words like, xanthan/zantan;exam/egzam; expect/ekspek)

In Patwa, the reader needs to pay keen attention to the sounds of words which may impact the spelling. For example, some words with **ear, er**, **ir, ur** sound, are replaced with **or**. Words such as, early, rehearsal and search are spelt in Patwa as, orli, riorsal, and sorch. Energy, nervous and superb, will become, enorji, norvos and suuporb. Also, circus, firm and stir will become sorkos, form and stor. Finally, disturb, pursue and urgent will become distorb, porsuu and orjent.

Another element to the Patwa writing style is that there is the combining, pairing, and mixing of the English vowels to represent the long vowel sounds in Patwa. See the examples below:

A = ie; **E** = ii; **I** = ai; **O** =uo; **U** =uu.

A=ie:

In writing Patwa, words such as bake, cake, name, pain, and same, are written as biek, kiek, niem, pien, siem where the English **a** is replaced with the long vowel, **ie.**

E=ii:

Words such as eat, meet, need, peel, and tea, use the long vowel **ii** in Patwa to replace the English **ee** or **ea.** Thus, the above words are written in Patwa as iit, miit, niid, piil and tii.

I=ai:

Words with the English **i** as in bite, find, like, time and write are written in Patwa as bait, fain, laik, taim and rait where the long vowel **ai** is used instead of just the **i**.

O=uo:

The English **o** as in cold, gold, know, road and show are written in Patwa as **uo** becoming kuol, guol, nuo, ruod and shuo. English words with **oo** are written in Patwa with **u** or **uu,** depending on whether it is a short or long vowel. For example, boot, food, good, mood, and shoot are written in Patwa as buut, fuud, gud, muud, and shuut. Although **good** has **oo**, it has a short vowel sound, so it is written as **gud** instead of **guud.** All the other words in the example have long vowel sounds, so the **uu** are used for them.

U=uu:

In Patwa, the single vowel **u** has a different sound from the double vowel **uu.** The single vowel **u** has a short sound, whereas the double vowel **uu** has a long sound. Here are some examples:

Single vowel **u**: book, good, look, should, stood, and wood in English are spelt in Patwa as, buk, gud, luk, shud, stud, and wud,

Double vowel **uu**: *boot, food, mood, root, blue, glue, fruit,* and *juice* in English are spelt in Patwa as, buut, fuud, muud, ruut, bluu, gluu, fruut, and juus.

In this example, we recognize that the 8 words with the combined vowels of **oo, ue,** and **ui**, in English, would be pronounced with a long sound. In Patwa the pronunciation would be the same, but the spelling would be different because, **uu** would replace **oo, ue**, and **ui**.

Patwa is a very expressive language that gives life and feelings to words. As a result, the author tries to capture and transfer the essence of the Jamaican lilting voice in some words through the use of blends.

Note: In the example that follows, a dash is used to separate the additional vowel which is used to explain the lilting sound in the word. (Lilting sound has a rhythm in the pronunciation of the word, as it rises and falls in a pleasant way).

Example

Word	**Patwa**	**Lilting sound**
Rejoice	rijais	rija-ais
Employ	emplai	empla-ai
Day	die	di-ie
Pray	prie	pri-ie

To help you understand and learn Patwa in a very simple way, this book covers the alphabet and outlines the various parts of speech which are the essential tools to navigate the language. Let us begin with the instructions in the **Quick Guide**, then we will continue with the letters of the alphabet and their usage.

Classification of The Patwa Alphabet

A B Ch D E F G H I J K L
M N O P R S T U V W Y Z

Vowels

Short: **a,e,i,o,u**
Long: **ie,ii,ai,uo,uu**
Other: **aa, ou**

Consonants

Regular: **b,d,f,g,h,j,k,l,m**
n,p,r,s,t,v,w,y,z
Other: **ch, ng, sh, zh**
Additional symbols: **or, hn.**

QUICK GUIDE

The following suggestions will prove useful in your study of the Patwa Language:

1. Listen carefully to Patwa speakers to have your ears trained, and practice the pronunciations.

2. Carefully study the Patwa vowels and consonants and use them as a guide to spell the words.

3. Patwa words are spelt based on how they are pronounced.

4. Study the Patwa Subject Verb structure. It is different, in some ways, from the English Language structure.

5. Study the Verb Tenses, and practice the accompanying activities.

6. Study the Personal Pronouns, Forming Plurals and the Word List given.

DI JAMIEKAN PATWA ALFIBETIKAL SISTIM

Di Jamiekan Patwa Alfibetikal Sistim is di aat a di Jamiekan Langwij. It is comparable in several ways to the English Language system, but there are some complex differences in pronunciations and expressions, making it uniquely Jamaican.

The English alphabet has 26 letters comprised of 21 consonants and 5 vowels, and the Patwa alphabet uses 24 of those 26 letters, but in a different way, to capture its unique sounds. Variation in the Patwa alphabet is evidenced by the 18 single-letter consonants and 4 double-letters which are formed from the already existing 18; plus, the 5 single and 7 double-letter vowels, as well as, 2 additional pair of double-letter symbols which give other sounds. The alphabets are comprised of vowels and consonants and are the major components of both the English and Patwa languages.

VOWELS

According to the Cambridge Dictionary, "a vowel is a sound which is produced by humans when the breath flows out through the mouth without being blocked by the teeth, tongue, or lips." Unlike English which uses five vowels to form words, Patwa uses those same five vowels along with some additional ones, as we shall see later in our lessons.

Here are the five letters **a, e, i, o, u** which are the symbols used to represent vowels in both English and Patwa to form words. Words contain sounds and are made up of syllables. To read and spell a new word, it is much easier to break it into syllables. A syllable is a part of a word containing sounds with at least one vowel. The vowels have similar expressions that can be short or long, depending on the usage. Let us examine the short vowel sounds more closely.

SHORT VOWEL SOUNDS

A short vowel sound occurs when the vowel is pronounced in a quick way. In English the short vowels are: a, e, i, o, u.

They are pronounced with the mouth opened, not blocked as in consonant, allowing the air to flow freely. Examples of short vowels seen in the following words: d**a**d, b**e**d, s**i**t, c**op**, c**u**t. Short vowels at times, may be the only vowel in a word, such as, the letters **A** and **I**, which can stand on their own. Example: **I** am **a** teacher. Short vowels may come at the beginning of a word, between two consonants, or at the end of the word.

Below, are five English and Patwa words, each beginning with one of the 5 vowels.

English	**Patwa**
Apple	Apl
Elbow	Elbo
Insect	Insek
Olive	Oliv
Umpire	Umpaiya

Did you pick up that short, crisp sound in each vowel? Here is a simple rule to help you identify the short vowel sound in English: If there is one vowel in a word at the beginning or between two consonants, usually this is a short vowel sound, but it may also come at the end of a word. **Notice** that the word *usually* is used because in English, certain vowels are irregular and do not comply with the rules for short and long vowels. Patwa is a bit more disciplined with the rules for short and long vowels.

LONG VOWEL SOUNDS

A long vowel sound occurs when the vowel is pronounced with a slight holding of that specific vowel by getting it to call its name. In English, the same letters, **a, e, i, o, u** are used for both short and long vowels, but in Patwa, the long vowels are written differently.

Patwa uses **aa, ii, uu** to represent three long vowel sounds, and **ie, ai, uo** and **ou** to express double vowel sounds in words. All these seven vowels are double-letter vowels. However, for simplicity in learning the Patwa language, the author has listed five of them as long vowels because they have similar sounds to the ones in the English Language, whereas, the remaining two have other unique sounds.

Let us examine the long vowels together:

IE, II, AI, UO, UU

Now, let us match these vowels with some words to bring out the sounds.

English	Patwa
April	**Ei**pril
Easter	**Ii**sta
Ice	**Ai**s
Over	**Uo**va
U(who)	**Uu**

Did you observe the difference in how these words are spelt in Patwa and in English? Despite major differences in spelling, the pronunciations are similar.

The remaining two vowels, **aa** and **ou** have unique sounds. **Aa** caries a long sound which is like the sound we hear when a doctor tells us to open our mouth wide, and we say augh! Here are some examples for you: all, talk, pause are English words which will become, aal, taak, paaz, in Patwa. Ou, on the other hand, has a slight lilt in pronunciation which can be likened to the sound we make when expressing pain, such as, ouch! Here are some examples for you: now, stout, town. These words will change to the Patwa spelling and will become, nou, stout, toun. However, they should be pronounced like their English counterpart.

GUIDE TO PRONOUNCING LONG VOWELS

Words	Sounds	Patwa
A=ie		
Date	di-ay-t	d**ie**t
Baby	bi-ay-bi	b**ie**bi
Pain	pi-ay-n	p**ie**n
Stay	st-i-ay	st**ie**
Weight	wi-ay-t	w**ie**t
E=ii		
Steam	st-ii-m	st**ii**m
Crème	kr-ii-m	kr**ii**m
Esteem	es-t-ii-m	est**ii**m
Receive	ri-sii-v	ris**ii**v
Fierce	f-ii-r-s	f**ii**rs
I=ai		
Item	ai-tem	**ai**tem
Identify	ai-den-ti-fai	**ai**dentif**ai**
Bicycle	b-ai-sikl	b**ai**sikl
Reply	ri-pl-ai	ripl**ai**
Silent	s-ai-lent	s**ai**lent
O=uo		
Road	r-uo-d	r**uo**d
Compose	kom-p-uo-z	komp**ou**z
Moment	m-uo-ment	m**uo**ment

Provoke	pro-v-uo-k	prov**uo**k
Vote	v-uo-t	v**uo**t

U=uu

Rule	r-uu-l	r**uu**l
Brew	br-uu	br**uu**
Food	f-uu-d	f**uu**d
Tool	t-uu-l	t**uu**l
Glue	gl-uu	gl**uu**

CONSONANTS

As previously mentioned, the English alphabet has 21 consonants and 5 vowels, whereas Patwa has 18 single-letter consonants plus, 4 double-letters which are formed from the already existing 18. Patwa also has 5 single and 7 double-letter vowels, in addition to 2 paired-letters which give other sounds. Even with so many vowels and combination of consonants, there are only 24 symbols in the Patwa alphabet.

The 18 single-letter Patwa consonants are: B, D, F, G, H, J, K, L, M, N, P, R, S, T, V, W, Y, Z, and the 4 double-letter consonants are: CH, NG, SH, ZH.

Both the Patwa and English sounds are similar.

Example as in:

B=ba	N=na
D=da	P=pa
F=fa	R=ra
G=ga	S=sa
H=ha	T=a
J=ja	V=va

K=ka	W=wa
L=la	Y=ya
M=ma	Z=za

MAJOR CHANGES BETWEEN THE ENGLISH AND PATWA ALPHABETS

There are some major changes between English and Patwa, affecting the way words are spelt and pronounced. We will discuss six of these changes which will help us to read and write Patwa more effectively.

1. The letter c

- This is **not** listed as a stand-alone part of the Patwa alphabet. Instead, it is used along with the letter **h** to form **ch**, one of the 24 letters of the Patwa alphabet. You will recognize the combined **ch** letter words, such as, choose, change, charity and chest.

- Where the soft sound **c** is used to form words in English, such as ceiling, cell, decent, entice, face and ice, in Patwa, the letter **s** is substituted. So, in Patwa, these words would become:

siilin, sel, diisent, entais, fies and ais.

2. **The letter k** has many functions as shown below:

   - **K** replaces the English hard sounding letter **c,** in Patwa.

     Example:

     come/kom
     company/kompini
     continue/kantinyu

   - It represents itself in the Patwa alphabet as, **k**.

     Example:

     kind/kain
     keep/kip
     kingdom/kindom

   - **K** combines with **w** to form another sound (see below).

3. **The letter q** is **not** included in the Patwa alphabet. To achieve the **q sound, k** links with **w** to become **kw**.

Thus, in Patwa, all English words with the letter **q** is written as **kw**.

Example:

quiet/kwaiat
quit/kwit
square/skwier

4. **The letter x** is also **not** included in the Patwa alphabet. Instead, the letter **z**, or a combination of other letters such as **gz** or **ks** are used to form words to replace the **x**, depending on the sound of the word itself.

   Example:

   xylophone/zailafuon
   exist/egzis
   exit/egzit
   x-ray/ekstrie

5. **Double-letter consonants** are letters of the alphabet that are paired together to bring about a particular sound in Patwa. They are **ch, ng, sh, zh**.

   - Each double letter has a particular sound that is similar to the sound in words that are in the English language. Both **ch** and **sh** function at the beginning, the middle and at the end of a word; while **ng** operates in the middle of a word and as a suffix. However, **zh** is used mostly as a suffix but it can operate as a prefix. Example: **zhoosh**.

- The following examples are presented in English and in Patwa.

Example 1

English
ch chop, champion, chest
lunchbox, peaches, catcher
beach, pitch, coach, preach
Patwa
ch chap, champyan, ches
lonchbaks, piichis, kctcha
biich, pitch, kuoch, priich

Example 2

English
sh short, share, shepherd
fashion, seashore, sunshine
goldfish, demolish, crash

Patwa
sh shaat, shier, shepod
fashan, siishuor sonshain
goulfish, dimalish, krash

Example 3
English
ng singe, finger, stronger
agonizing, baking, using
Patwa
ng sinj, fingga, chrangga
aganaizin, biekin, yuuzin

Example 4
English
zh decision, version,
illusion, conversion
Patwa
zh disizhan, vorzhan,
iluuzhan, konvorzhan

Let us again examine **zh**, but this time, we will dissect the English words above with the suffix **sion** to determine why it is different from the other examples. Unlike the previous examples, **ch, ng** and **sh** are included in the spelling of the English words; but not the **zh**. Patwa words are spelt phonetically, according to the sound of the English words.

However, the English suffix **sion** has a **zhan** sound, which is transferred into the Patwa spelling, but not the English spelling.

Did you pick up that **zh** sound in the word *version*? It represents itself in the suffix **sion**, the Patwa equivalent being **zhan**. **Zh** has a slight inflection in pronunciation, a sound that is similar in words, such as, *confusion, decision,* and *television*; or kanfuuzhan, disizhan, telivizhan.

In Patwa, not all words ending with *sion* are spelt with **zh**. Words, such as, tension, ascension, and comprehension are spelt with **shan** because of the difference in pronunciation; hence, *tenshan, asenshan,* and *komprienshan*.

Note: Words ending with **tion** are also spelt with **shan** in Patwa because of the sound.

6. **The Combo Hn**
   Here is the final combination of letters **Hn,** used to express the **aahn** sound. **Hn** has a nasal sound in words such as, want/**waahn** and cant't/ **kyaahn**.

Here are some ways in which **hn** is used in sentences.

Example:

a) *Wa a gwaahn?*
What's happening? How are you? What's up?

b) *Im waahn fi sliip.*
He wants to sleep.

c) *Mi kyaahn dwiit til maanin.*
I cannot do it until in the morning.

ESSENTIAL TOOLS

English Language in its structure, incorporates eight parts of speech as essential tools. They are: noun, pronoun, verb, adjective, adverb, preposition, conjunction and interjection. The Jamiekan Patwa also uses these eight parts of speech as essential tools. Let us begin with Verbs.

VERBS

To prevent, or at least reduce chaos in life, there has to be some kind of structure. We see this every day on the roads, in the way people drive and navigate their spaces. Similarly, for us to communicate effectively with each other, there has to be some form of structure.

A verb operates just like a traffic light or a stop sign on the road by providing action. It tells us when to go and when to stop; when to turn and when to make a detour. Simply, the verb tells us the action to take.

Before continuing further with verbs, let me introduce a very essential component of communication, the subject and object, which work with verbs.

- **Subject and Object:**

In speech we need to talk about people, places, and things that make the conversation easy to understand. The subject can be about the name of a person, animal, place, or thing, while the object is always the person or the thing receiving the action.

- **Subject Verb Agreement**

We construct sentences with a subject, a verb and an object. The subject can be about the name of a person, animal, place, or thing; the verb tells us about the action or state of the subject. The subject is the main part of the sentence; the object is the person or the thing that receives the action of the verb. In English, all three of these must agree, hence we have what is called Subject Verb Agreement. For instance: If the subject is singular, the verb must be singular too. And, if the subject is plural, the verb must also be plural.

Example 1

The girl **sings** every morning.

Example 2

They **sing** every morning.

Notice that in example 1, it talks about one girl who is the subject in the sentence, and it uses the singular form of the verb **sings.** Therefore, the subject and the verb agree. In example 2, it talks about more than one person, and it uses the plural form of the verb **sing.** Therefore, the subject and the verb agree.

Now, let us observe carefully how the sentence structure works in Patwa. Although it has a subject verb sentence structure like in English, it is **different,** because the verb does not change with the subject in Patwa.

Here is an example to demonstrate how the verb **like** functions in Patwa, as shown in the chart that follows.

Example

ENGLISH		**PATWA**	
Subject	**Verb**	**Subject**	**Verb**
I	like	Mi	like
He	likes	Im	like

She	likes	Shi	like
It	likes	Ee , i, it	like
You	like	Yu	like
We	like	Wi	like
They	like	Dem	like
You (aal)	like	Unu	like

Notice in the example that, I, he, she, it are singular subjects. Whereas, we, they, and you (*referring to more than one*) are plural subjects. However, I and you (*singular*), always take the plural form of the verb. This is the general rule in English. But, in Patwa, the situation is different because the verb never changes; it remains constant.

Activity

Use the word believe along with the subjects that are given to complete the activity in the chart below. Follow the format as shown in the previous example.

ENGLISH	**PATWA**
I	
You	

He	
She	
It	
We	
They	
You	

- **Verb Tenses**

A verb tense is determined by the action of the verb, and, in the English Language there are different types of verb tenses which determine the activity. For example, the most frequently used verb tenses are: present, past, and future tenses.

(a) The present tense tells us what is happening;

(b) The past tense tells what has already happened;

(c) The future tense tells us what will happen;

- **Present Tense and Copula**

In English a copula is a word or a phrase that links or connects the subject of a sentence to a subject complement. The subject complement completes the meaning of the topic being discussed. Usually, the verb **to be** is the *linking word or phrase* used to describe someone or something. The **to be** verb is very irregular and is written according to the subject, or the tense: present, past, or future tense.

In Patwa, the verb remains constant but it is influenced by the introduction of a word that is put in front of it, which changes the tense. To make a sentence in Patwa into the present tense, a linking word known as a **copula** is used. The copula supports the verb, and in Patwa the letter **a** is the copula which is used as the participle for the continuous tense.

Let us now take a look at **copula** and how it is used in the construction of sentences in English as compared to Patwa.

Example:

1. I am looking for you.

Mi a luk fi yu.

2. You are coming with me.

   Yu a kom wid mi.

3. He is dancing with her.

   Im a daans wid ar.

Did you observe the difference between the sentence structure in English and the sentence structure in Patwa? Unlike the English Language where the sentence has a subject verb agreement pattern, the Jamiekan Patwa has none.

In the Patwa sentences the verbs remain constant, and the copula **a** is used to support the verbs. The copula **a** is so important that I want you to look at another example in the chart that follows. Just by adding the copula **a** before the verb, the present tense is formed and the Patwa verb remains the same, even when the subject is changed from a singular to a plural form.

Example

ENGLISH	PATWA
I am dancing	Mi a daans
You are looking	Yu a luk
He is talking She is singing	Im a taak/chat Shi a sing
It is ringing	Ee/i a ring
We are hurting	Wi a ort
They are working	Dem a wok
You are laughing	Unu a laaf

Here is an activity for you. Rewrite the sentences in Patwa, using the **copula a.**

Sentences:

1. I am teaching Patwa.

----

2. You are using the telephone.

----

3. He is thinking about her.

----

4. She is taking her son with her.

----

5. It is landing now.

----

6. We are jogging on the beach.

----

7. They are standing in the way.

----

8. You are searching for the dog.

Did you notice that the copula **a** function as the support for each verb?

- **Past Tense**

The Past Tense in Jamiekan Patwa is formed by adding the word **did** to the sentence, as shown in the chart that follows.

Example

SENTENCES Pres. Tense	**ENGLISH** Past Tense	**PATWA** P. Tense
I come	I came	Mi **did** kom
You go	You went	Yu **did** gu
He looks	He looked	Im **did** luk
She walks	She walked	Shi **did** waak
It jumps	It jumped	It **did** jump
We pray	We prayed	Wi **did** prie
They love	They loved	Dem **did** lov

You preach	You preached	Aal a yu **did** priich or Unu did priich

Here is an activity for you to practice what you have learned about forming past tense.

Activity

Fill in the blank spaces in the chart to complete the activity.

SENTENCES Pres. Tense	**ENGLISH** Past Tense	**PATWA** Past Tense
I agree		
You appear		
He announces		
She amuses		
It annoys		
We belong		
They borrow		
You change		

How well did you do? Did you follow the rules by using the word **did** to form the past tense in Patwa?

Note: Depending on where you are in Jamaica, "ben" or "en" can also be added to form the past tense.

- **Future Tense**

In English there are four types of future verb tenses. They are the simple future tense, the future continuous tense, the future perfect tense, and the future perfect continuous tense. In this book consideration will be given to the Simple Future Tense.

The *Simple Future Tense* is a verb tense that is used to talk about things before they happen or things that are about to take place. In English, the word *will* or *shall* is used to form the simple future tense.

To write the future tense in Patwa the words **a gu** are used to support the verb, as you will see in the following example.

Example

ENGLISH	**PATWA**
I will be shopping on-line tomorrow	Mi **a gu** shap pan lain tumaaro
You will play football in the park	Yu **a gu** plie futbaal in a di paak
He will do his exam on Friday	Im **a gu** du im egzam pan Fraide
She will act in the movie on Saturday	Shi **a gu** ak ina wan muovi pan Satde
We will help him with his homework	Wi **a gu** elp im wid im uomwok
They will rehearse their new song tonight	Dem **a gu** ri-ors dem nyuu sang tinait
You will perform on stage next week Sunday	Yu **a gu** porfaam pan stiej neks wiik Sonde

Activity

Rewrite the sentences in Patwa, and use the words **a gu** to form the future tense.

ENGLISH	**PATWA**
I will go with you	
You will know the truth soon	
He will walk you home later	
She will call you tomorrow	
We will drive with you in your car	
They will host the Reggae Festival on Saturday	
You will get stronger	

How well did you do? Did you notice that all the verbs in the Patwa sentences remain constant?

PRONOUNS

A pronoun takes the place of a noun. There are different types of pronouns but for simplicity of our discussion, we will focus on personal pronouns.

Personal Pronouns

A personal pronoun is used in place of a specific noun for a person, place or thing, and it helps the sentence to flow without being repetitious. It identifies the person or thing as singular or plural, gender specific, first, second or third person.

In English, personal pronouns are also divided into three cases: subjective, objective, and possessive.

Subject Pronoun takes the place of the subject and includes **I, you, he, she, it, we, you, they.**

Object Pronoun stands in for a noun that is the object of that sentence and it includes **me, you, him, her, it, us, you, them**.

Possessive Pronoun shows ownership, and it includes **mine, yours, his, hers, its, ours, yours, theirs.**

The possessive pronoun in Patwa is formed by merely adding **fi** in-front of the pronoun. Example: fi mi buk, fi mi lunch, fi unu yaad, fi unu kyaar, fi dem kat and fi dem bwai pikni. Also, **a fi** could be used, such as, "a fi mi buk" or "a fi unu yaad" or "a fi dem kyaar"; all showing ownership.

*Not*e: Patwa does not use the apostrophe **s** to show ownership.

Comparing Personal Pronouns Between English and Patwa

Let us examine the following chart to show the differences between the subject and object pronouns in English, and how they compare with Patwa.

Eng. (Singular)	**Patwa** (Singular)	**Eng.** (Plural)	**Patwa** (Plural)
1ST Person			
I, me	Mi	We, us	Wi
2nd Person			
You	Yu	You	Unu
3rd Person			
He, him She, her It, it	Im Shi, ar i	They/ them You/you	Dem

As seen in the chart above, English usually uses a different pronoun for the subject and the object. Most personal pronouns in Patwa resemble English pronouns, but Patwa keeps it really simple by using the same pronoun for both subject and object.

Below are some of the differences and similarities of the pronouns between English and Patwa:

- First person pronoun (singular): English uses **I** (subject) and **me** (object) and Patwa uses **mi** for both subject and object.

- First person pronoun (plural): English uses **we** (subject) and **us** (object), but Patwa uses **wi** for both.

- Second person pronoun in English deviates and uses the same pronoun **you** for both singular and plural, subject and object, and gender, just like the Patwa, **yu**.

- Third person pronouns in English are a bit more complex with both singular and plural pronouns, subject and object pronouns, and gender specific pronouns, except with the inanimate pronoun **it,** which can be used for either male or female.

- The pronoun, **him** (English) is **im** in Patwa and is used for both male and female. Other third person singular Patwa pronouns are **shi** (she), **ar** (her) and **i** (it).

Note: **im** is the most frequently third person pronoun (singular) that is used in writing and speaking Patwa.

Adopt this simple rule: Patwa usually uses 3 singular pronouns, **mi, yu, im** and 3 plural pronouns, **wi, unu, dem**. However, there are variations to this rule, and those are also correct.

FORMING PLURALS

In English, plurals are generally constructed by adding **s** or **es** to the nouns, but in Patwa, they are formed differently. Most plurals in Patwa are formed by adding words, such as, **dem, nof, plenti,** and **uoliip,** as well as using **a number** to denote the quantity.

- **Dem** is used after the singular noun to make it into the plural form.

  Example: boy, car, man, manggo, and pot will become the plural forms in Patwa as bwai dem, kyaar dem, man dem, manggo dem and pat dem.

  When dem is used after a proper name, it conveys not just the person listed, but others, such as **Daniel dem**, which means Daniel and others.

  Dem appears to be the most widely used word to form plurals in Patwa.

- **Nof, plenti and uoliip** are used before the noun to convert it into the plural form.

  Example: The singular form of apple, crab, egg, banana, crayon and pear can be converted into the plural forms by using either nof or plenti, such as nof apl, nof krab, nof eg; plenti banana, plenti kriaan, and plenti piir.

- **Uoliip** is often used to emphasize a very large quantity.

  Example: A fisherman with a very large catch may say "Mi ketch uoliip a fish." Also, doubling or tripling the nof and plenti (nof nof or plenti plenti plenti) commonly denotes an unusually large quantity. For gross exaggeration, more nof and plenti can be added. This exaggeration is normally conveyed with a rising in the voice with each plenti or nof, just like a crescendo.

- A **number** can also be used before the noun to form the plural. For example,

6 buk, 10 konchri, 8 daag, 12 ous, and 15 jiip.

- The **letter z** can also be added at the end of some Patwa nouns to form the plural.

  Example: die/diez, prablem/prablemz, ting/tingz, slang/slangz.

Activity

Rewrite the sentences below in Patwa, using **dem, nof, plenti, uoliip** to form the plural. Use each word in at least two of the sentences.

Note: All 4 words convey similar meaning. So, there is no *absolute* right or wrong answer to this activity.

Sentences:

1. The dogs barked and ran after the boys.

2. We have several things to do tomorrow.

3. The students will be travelling to Kingston with their teachers on Thursday.

4. We can see several birds flying in the sky.

5. Where are the children going to play if it rains?

6. The Reid's will be moving out of town on Saturday.

7. We had lots and lots of drinks at the party last night.

8. We need many hands to come on deck if we are to complete the project on time.

9. The girls got lost while shoe-shopping in the city.

10. There are 12 oranges left in the bag to share for all of you.

How well did you do with this activity?

PRONUNCIATION

Pronunciation is the way a word is spoken, and it can be done in various ways by different individuals. New learners of a language normally sound different from native speakers until they grasp certain concepts and with time and practice conquer the language.

Patwa is a very expressive language and exudes a vocal attitude of rhythmic beat evolved from English, Spanish and West African languages with a sprinkling of Hindi, Dutch and Portuguese. Patwa pronunciations will differ throughout the island and among different groups, but the meanings generally remain the same and so there should be no difficulty in communicating.

Rules governing the pronunciation and grammar are different in Patwa than in standard English, as it is more relaxed and informal in expression. The spellings in Patwa tend to be more phonetic since for many years it was mostly a spoken language without a standardized written format. There are variations in spelling Patwa words, but as mentioned previously, the Patwa words in this book are based on Cassidy – JLU Writing System.

The reader is encouraged to listen keenly to the spoken Patwa, and to learn the rhythmic beat of the language by paying attention to the intonation (rise and fall of the voice) and modulation (variation in the pitch, pace, and power of the voice). In Patwa, both the intonation and modulation create a sing-song style, resulting in that special musical flair which readily identifies the spoken language as Jamaican Patwa. Also, the intonation and modulation express emotions and attitudes, and when Jamaicans speak there is a tendency to convey strong feelings by painting vocally, a colourful language.

The author wants you to try and isolate certain syllables in words, or certain words in a sentence, and copy the rhythmic sounds of the native Patwa speakers. One way to learn to pronounce Patwa words is to study the vowels as they are the anchor of the language. In Patwa, the short vowels are similar to the English ones; **a, e, i, o, u**, but the long vowels are different, and when combined there are 12 of them, each of which was previously covered under the caption **Vowels.**

In English the letter **h**, more often than not, is pronounced whether used at the beginning or between words. It carries a puff sound, except in words, such as, heir, honest, hour, ghost, ghetto, rhyme, where it remains silent.

While most Patwa speakers *do not* use the stand-alone **h** in writing or in pronouncing words, some do over-emphasize the **h** by adding it where there is none. For example, egg becomes **hegg,** and alphabet becomes **halfibet.** Our use of **h** will focus on combining it with the letter **c** to form the consonant diagraph **ch**, which in itself carries the **ch** sound as in chair, beach, kitchen.

Certain English words ending in **d** such as **and, end**, **bend, lend** and **send**, are not pronounced in Patwa and are written as **an**, **en**, **ben**, **len**, and **sen**.

The letter **g** in words ending with **ing** is sometimes not pronounced in Patwa, as is shown in the following examples: bringing, laughing, painting, running, singing, talking, walking, writing. In Patwa these would be: *bringin, laafin, pientin, ronin, singin, taakin, waakin, raitin.*

The diagraph th

In Patwa, the diagraph **th** plays a major role in the pronunciation and like a caterpillar, it changes into a beautiful butterfly when the concept is thoroughly grasped. Let us take a look at the example which follows to see how the **th** sounding words are usually written in English.

The English **th** is written at the beginning of the word, in the middle or at the end. It gives a soft or hard sound.

Examples of soft sound **th** are: thunder, thin, thorn, thirteen; bathroom, earthquake, healthy; growth, month, width.

Examples of hard sound **th** are: this, that, them, there, though, they, thus, feather, further, breathe, neither.

Patwa has no **th** word or sound. It changes the English **th** into either **d** or **t** as seen in the following.

Example:

English:

a) the, this, that, them, thing, think

b) mother, father, brother, other

c) length, tenth, cloth, with, both

Patwa:

a) di, dis, dat, dem, ting, tingk

b) mada, faada, breda, ada

c) lent, tent, klaat, wit, buot

Here now is an activity for you to see how well you have grasped the concept.

Activity: Write the Patwa equivalent to the English words given in the chart.

ENGLISH	PATWA
Anything Athlete Breathless Brethren Earthquake	

Either	
Faithful	
Growth	
Thank	
Think	
Three	
Tooth	
Within	

Other Sounds

Word-endings that change in Patwa

English words ending in **ar, er, or, ur, ure** are frequently replaced in Patwa with the vowel **a** as seen in the example below.

Example:

pill**ar**/pilla
comput**er**/kompuuta
direct**or**/direkta
sulf**ur**/solfa
pict**ure**/pikcha

The double vowel, aa

In English, **ar** and **or** occurring between two consonants are substituted in Patwa by the double vowels, **aa**.

Example:

apart/apaat	fork/faak
sharp/shaap	cork/kaak
park/paak	short/shaat
yard/yaad	storm/staam

Words beginning with sm and sn

In Patwa, there are two distinctive sounds when **s** is used before the letters **m** and **n** at the beginning of words. Although not widespread, these sounds may be heard among some Jamaicans.

In cases where the letter **s** comes before the letter **m,** the vowel **u** is inserted between the two letters, giving a different sound.

Example:

smoke/sumuok
small/sumaal

smooth/sumuud
smart/sumaat

Some English words beginning with **sn** have the vowel **i** inserted between the **s** and **n**, resulting in a different Patwa pronunciation.

Example:

sneeze/siniiz
sneeking/siniikin
snowball/sinuobaal
snapshot/sinapshot

When Ttl/tl and Ddl/dl are replaced by another letter

Sometimes, in Patwa the letters **ttl/tl** are replaced by **kl**; and **ddl/dl** by **gl**.

Example 1

little/likl	gentle/genkl
bottle/bakl	title/taikl
kettle/kekl	turtle/torkl

Example 2

middle/migl	candle/kyanggl
saddle/sagl	bridle/braigl
fiddle/figl	bundle/bonggl

Here are two other sounds for you to learn well. They are presented in words with the combined letters of **tr** and **dr**. As a result, in Patwa **tr** words are spelt with the letters **ch** and are pronounced with the **ch** sound. Whereas, words with **dr** are spelt with **j** in front of them. Hence the pronunciation begins with a **j sound**. Let's look at some examples:

Tr changes to ch sound

Track, train, trick, truck, trust, truth, traffic, trap, trouble; central, control, citrus, metric, patrol, petrol.

The spelling of these words in Patwa would as follows: chak, chien, chik, chok, chos, chuut, chafik, chap, chobl, senchal, kanchuol, sichos, mechik, pachuol, pechal.

Dr words with j sound

Dragon, drama, dress, drop, drink, drive, drugs, drunk; address, syndrome.

These words are spelt as they are pronounced in Patwa: jdragan, jdraama, jdres, jdrap, jdringk, jdraiv, jdrogz, jrongk; ajdres, sinjdruom.

Note however, that some of these **dr** words are sometimes pronounced differently by some Patwa speakers. Example: drink (jingk); drugs (jogz).

AFN YUUZ WOD DEM

English	Patwa
all	aal
and	an
another	aneda
ask	aks
be	bi
because	bikaaz/kaaz
before	bifou
but	bot
can	kyan
cannot	kyaan
car	kyaar
catch	ketch
certificate	sorfitikit
chat	chat/taak
church	choch
come	kom/kum
continue	kantinyu
could	kud/kuda
country	konchri/konchi
different	difrant
do	du
down	dung

dynamite	dandimait
eat	nyaam
english	ingglish
earring	erring/eizring
film	flim
for	fi
forget	figet
from	fram
funeral	finaral
future	fyuucha
get	git
give	gi
go	go/gu
happen	apm
have	av
he	im
her	ar
here	iir
him	im
his	iz
how	ou
hundred	onjrid
if	ef
just	jos
know	nuo

listen	lisn
little	likl/likkl
long	lang
look	luk
make	mek
me	mi
military	militri
no	nuo/naa
not	nat/naa
nothing	notn
number	nomba
of	af
old	oul
on	pan
only	onggl
or	ar
other	ada
our	oua
over	uova
pudding	pudn
safety	siefiti
secretary	sekiteri
see	si
she	shi
should	shud/shuda

something	sopm/sitn/sinting
that	dat
the	di
them	dem
then	den
there	diir
they	dem
think	tingk/tink
this	dis
thorn	maka
those	duoz
though	dou
thousand	touzn
three	chrii
through	chuu
to	tu/to
tomato	tumatis
up	op
us	os
water	waata
we	wi
what	wa
when	wen
where	we
who	uu

ELPFUL WOD LIS

abuse	abyuuz
according	askaadn/azkaadn
although	alduo
alright	aarait
always	aalwiez
believe	biliiv
bible	baibl
bird	bod
blessing	blesn
boil	bwail
bondage	bandij
brother	brada/breda
burn	bon
burst	bos
bury	beri
capture	kyapcha
care	kier
carry	kyari
change	chienj
charge	chaaj
christian	kristiyan
church	choch
coming	komin

community	komyuuniti
company	kompni
concern	kansorn
confuse	kanfuuz
congregation	kanggrigieshan
continue	kantinyu
control	kanchoul
cope	kuop
corner	kaana
connect	kanek
correct	karek
cover	kova
create	kriyiet
creation	kriyieshan
creator	kriyieta
creole	kriyuol
cruel	kruwil
day	die
decision	disijan
deserve	dizorv
destroy	dischrai
devil	devl
different	difrant
doctrine	dakchrin
donate	duoniet

done	don
don’t	duohn
down	dong
download	dongluod
draw	jraa
dream	jriim
drink	jringk
drunk	jongk
drop	jrap
dry	jrai
earth	ort
earthquake	ortkwiek
easy	iizi
eat	iit/nyaam
education	edikieshan
encourage	inkorij
enough	nof
everybody	evribadi
exactly	egzakli
experience	ekspiiriyens
explain	eksplien
family	fambili
figure	figa
fire	faiya
first	fos

flood	flod
food	fuud
foot	fut
force	fuos
forgive	figiv
forward	faawod
future	fyuucha
gather	gyada
garden	gyaadn
generation	jinarieshan
giant	jaiant
gone	gaan
guidance	gaidans
happiness	apinis
hard	aad
healthy	elti
heart	aat
humble	ombl
hungry	onggri
husband	ozban
important	impuotant
justice	jostis
language	langwij
learn	lorn
lessen	lesn

life	laif
like	laik
linger	lingga
isten	lisn
mango	manggo
marriage	marij
message	mesij
millions	miliyanz
mistake	mistiek
more	muo/muor
most	muos
move	muuv
much	moch
multiply	moltiplai
nation	nieshan
news	nyuuz
nice	nais
nobody	nobadi
now	nou
older	uola
only	onggl
opposite	opozit
organization	aaganaizieshan
page	piej
pain	pien

part	paat
people	piipl
picture	picha
plus	plos
point	paint
poison	paizn
practice	praktis
pray	prie
prayer	prieya
principle	prinsipl
proper	prapa
protect	pritek
public	poblik
quality	kwaliti
question	kwestiyan
really	riili
reason	riizn
recording	rekaadin
relationship	riliesllanship
resurrect	rezarek
right	rait
righteous	raichos
same	siem
scripture	skripcha
short	shaat

show	shuo
sister	sista
snake	siniek
society	sosaiyati
somebody	sumadi
special	speshal
stronger	schrangga
study	stodi
suffering	sofarin
support	sopuot
suppose	supuos
today	tide
together	tugeda
touch	toch
training	chrienin
translate	chransiliet
travel	chravl/chavl
treat	chriit
tree	chrii
trouble	chobl
true	chuu
truth	chuut
try	chrai/chai
turn	ton
under	anda

understand	andastan
unite	yuunait
video	vidyio
watch	wach
wise	waiz
witness	witnis
woman	uman
wont	wuohn
world	worl
worse	wos
worthless	woklis
write	rait
wrong	rang
year	iir

DAIALAG

D1 - AT WAN IIRPUOT IN A JAMIEKA

- **Anounsment a di iirpuot**

Liediz an jentlman dem, unu welkom to Jamieka, di lan a wud an waata. Wi api fi si aal a unu. Pliiz waak gud an go tek op unu bagij dem an prosiid to imigrieshan.

- **Outsaid a di Iirpuot**

Taksiman Taksi fi yu mam, we bout yu sa? Nais liedi yu waahn taksi?

Vizita Yes sa.

Taksiman Pliiz kom dis wie mam. A ou moch a unu a travl tugeda.

Vizita Chrii a wi.

Taksiman Ok. Mek mi tek di bagij dem fram unu an put dem ina di van

	bak. Unu go si dung an mek unuself komfatebl. Unu a go enjai di raid fram Mantiigo Bie to di otel.
Vizita	Tangk yu
Taksiman	Dem kaal mi Sala, an unu sief wid mi. A wich wan a di otel dem unu a go tu?
Vizita	Di Kwiinz in Chilaani.
Taksiman	Datz a nais wan. Unu a go enjai unuself. Ita go tek bout wan oua fram yaso fi go dung de, bot unu no afi wori, a lang taim mi a chavel pan dis ya ruut so mi nou di roningz. A di fos taim unu a kom ya?
Vizita	Yes.
Taksiman	Wel yu gwain lov i.

	Unu waah mi ton dong di winda dem so unu kyan enjai di nais Jamiekan briiz?
Vizita	O yes! Wi wuda lov dat.

- **Chavlin to di otel**

Taksiman	Wi draiv pan di lef in a fi wi konchi, so no get norvos if unu si mi a uovatek pan di rait.
Vizita	Ok Sala.
Taksiman	Luk pan di sii uova de so. Unu si ou i priti?
Vizita	It priti fi chuu.
Taksiman	Yes man, yu shuda siit a nait taim. A dat time i priti...wid aal di lait dem a shain jos laik piini waali! Unu nuo bout dat?

Vizita No. Wi no nuo bout dat. A we niem piini waali?

Taksiman A wan insek we de bout ya ina fi wi konchi, an dem av lait pan dem tiel an dem flai bout a nait an lait op di plies. Dem se di rait niem fi dem a faiya flai bot ina Jamieka wi kaal dem piini waali.

Vizita Wel, wi uop se wi kan si som a dem bifou wi lef ya.

Taksiman Aks di Belap bout i wen yu riich di otel. Im wi nuo.
Wel, wi a enta di prapati nou so unu suu riich di otel, an mi nou se unu a go enjai unuself.

- **Riich di otel**

Wi de ya now so mek mi tek di bagij dem outa di chongk fi unu.

Vizita Tangk yu Sala. Wi enjai di raid an di kanvasieshan.
Ou much a di fier?

Taksiman Dat a $85 mam.

Vizita Mi a go gi yu $100 an yu kyan kip di chienj.

Taksiman an di Belap

Taksiman Bwai, mi nuo se yu a go git wan fat tip fram dem piipl ya tide, kaaz a nof bagij dem av.

Belap Evriting kris man…nof rispek!

Taksiman Nais, a dat mi waahn iir.

D2 - Tuu Fren dem a Riizn

Frangk: We yu a se?

Brokop: Bwai mi naa se notn. Mi jos a kip kool kaaz dis ting kaal COVID a mash op mi pakit.

Frangk: A chuu. Taim aad.

Brokop: Yes man, an mi av di pikni dem fi main an mi naa wok. Bot mi av fait dat sopn a go apn suun. We yu tingk?

Frangk: Bwai it rof fi chuu, bot wi kyaahn gi op. So, we mi plan fi du is tu go plaant sopn fi nyaam in a di flouas pat dem.

Brokop: Dat soun gud man. Wi a get likl rien nou a diez, so sopn mos grou, iivn likl kaan.

D3 - Shapin in a wan Maakit

- **A di Maakit**

Kostama: Ou yu sel di manggo dem?

Igla: Wan a dem a fi \$3 an aaf dozn fi \$17. Mi wi gi yu 1 dozn fi \$30.

Kostama Mi wi tek 1 dozn a di manggo dem. Mek shuor yu gi mi dem 2 raip wan de.

Igla Wich wan dem dat?

Kostama Di tord an fuot wan fram di aki.

Igla Iir iz yu dozn.
Eluo nais liedi, yu waan som a di stanjariin an pepaswim dem. Mi aalso av pangranat an papaa.

Kostama Mi wi tek 2 bag a di pepaswim dem an a papaa.

Igla	Dat a gu bi faati-nain ($49) dala. Tortichii ($33) dala fi di pepaswim dem an sikstiin ($16) dala fi di papaa.
Kostama	Tangkyu. Neks-taim mi wi git di pangranat.

D4 - Restaraant

Wieta	Maanin. We mi kyan git yu tide Mis.
Kostama	Pliiz gi mi wan smaal aki brekfas wid fuud. Mi aalso waan 2 kadfish flitaz an a mug a kaafi.
Wieta	Dat is $22 aal tugeda. $12 fi di aki wid fuud, $6 fi di tuu flitas, an $4 fi di mug a kaafi. Kan mi sorv yu sopn fram di biekri?

Kostama	Yes, mi waah a kopkiek wid yalo aisin pan it.
Wieta	Dat a go bi $3 mou.
Kostama	Ok. Iir, an yu kyan kip di chienj.

PAPILA EKSPRESHANZ

Patwa	English
A no notn	It is ok
An migl	Hand middle
Baad	Gud
Bag-an-pan	Too much things
Bangarang	In trouble
Belibatam	belly
Big op	Rispek
Braata	Something extra
Bunununus	A nice person
Bwai pikni	A young boy
Chati-chati	Talk too much
Chuubi	Just because
Dash we	Throw away
Dege dege	One thing only
Di likl pikni	A small child
Dupi	Ghost
Dwiit	Do it
Fuon skriim	Phone screen
Fengke fengke	Weak
Fut-batam	Sole of foot
Fuulinish	Foolishness
Galang	Go on

Gi mi a blai	Do me a favour
Iez uol	Ear drum
Livity	Life/living
Megl megl	Busy-body/nosey
Moutamasi	Inquisitive
Nigaraitis	Doze after a meal
Nuoz uol	Nostril
Nyaami nyaami	Greedy
Osh	It will be ok
Red yai	Envious
Tan a yu yaad	Stay home
Tande	Stay there
Tan op	Stop, don't move
Wiil an kom agen	Start over…better
Yai baal	Eye ball
Yai waata	Tears
Yu a yaadi	Are you Jamaican?
Yu si mi	Do you understand

GRIITINZ & GUDBAIZ

1. Ou fi griit wananeda:

Oudi	Oudiduu
Maanin	Gud Maanin
Aftanuun	Gud Aftanuun
Iivnin	Gud Iivnin

Using a question:

Wa a gwaahn?	Waapn?
We yu a se?	Evriting kris?
Wats op?	Yu aarait?

2. Ou fi se gudbai

Lieta	Si yu tumaaro
Likl muo	Nait nait
Babai	Mi a lef nou
Tek kier	Mi a go we nou
Mi suun kom	Mi a tekwe miself

TIES DI JAMIEKAN KOLCHA

A unique way to understand some Jamaican culture is through **Jamiekan Pravorbs**. These are Patwa expressions using figurative language, and the meanings are profound! There are twelve of them that are listed here for you to decipher. The meanings are in brackets for you to check your answers.

1. Shuo mi yu kompini mi tel yu uu yu aar.
   (Di taip a fren wi chuuz wi ditormin wi karakta).

2. Wen trobl tek yu, pikni shut fit yu.
   (Wen smadi ina trobl, eni elp im get im tek it an ajos tu it).

3. Kak mout kil kak.
   (Kierful we yu se kaaz yu uon wod kyan bitrie yu, aar it kyan aant yu).

4. Oul faiya tik iizi fi ketch.
   (A ruomantik rilieshanship we gaan bad kyan iizili ketch bak).

5. Wan wan kuoko ful baaskit.
   (Ebri litl bit kount; dat is we wil mek di difrans in riichin di guol or taagit set).

6. Gud fren beta dan pakit moni.
   (Chreja yu fren dem kaaz a dem a go kom tu yu resku in taim af niid, nat yu richiz).

7. Tek we yu get til yu get we yu waahn
   (Satisfai wid we yu av kaaz uova taim it a go get beta).

8. No bai pus ina bag.
   (Chek di faks fos bifuo yu chuuz we fi du; or ties i fos).

9. Nuu bruum swiip kliin, bot oul bruum nuo di kaana.
   (Piipl shuda straiv fi a api miks bitwiin di oul an di nuu).

10. Waahnt aal luuz aal.
    (Wi no fi griidi. Tek we wi kyan manij an liiv som fi adaz so dat wi no spwail di gud rilieshanship wid dem).

11. Chikin meri aak de niir.
(Dienja de bout bot yu no rialaiz i).

12. Kyaahn ketch kwaaku, yu ketch im shot.
(Yu mait nat ketch uu yu waahn bot yu ketch smadi we bilang tu im).

JAMIEKAN SLANGZ

1. Wa a gwaahn?
   [How are you. What's going on; What is happening?]

2. Jamieka, nuo problem!
   [All is well…Everything is ok.]

3. Big op yuself!
   [Well done.]

4. Nof rispek!
   [To show honour, appreciation or to say thanks]

5. We yu se!
   [What did you say.]

6. Wc yu a sey!
   [What are you saying.]

7. We yu de?
   [Where are you?]

8. We de pan di menyu tide?
   [What is on the menu today?]

9. A uu fa sitn dat?
   [Whose something is that.]

10. Mi no nou.
    [I don't know.]

11. Yu a kom?
    [Are you coming?]

12. Mi naa kom.
    [I am not coming.]

13. Mi suun kom.
    [I will be there soon.]

14. Mi no waa da wan ya.
    [I don't want this one.]

15. Mi no waa da wan de.
    [I don't want that one.]

16. A uu se so!
    [Who said that?]

17. We mek yu tan so bad?
    [Why are you behaving so badly?]

18. Smaal op yuself.

[Move over and allow someone-else in the space.]

19. No mash i op!
    [Don't break it up!]

20. Kuya!
    [Look here!]

21. Mi de ya.
    [I am here.]

22. Tan de!
    [Stay there!]

23. Im fras uot.
    [To be tired or very drunk.]

24. Im trash uot.
    [A well-dressed person.]

JAIN DI KANVASIESHAN

This section captures some popular expressions that can help you to become more adept at speaking and writing Patwa.

To decipher these terms, a **key** is provided at the end of this section.

1. Wa a gwaahn?
2. Wa yu a du?
3. We yu a du ya?
4. A we yu a gu?
5. We yu liv?
6. We yu kaal mi fa?
7. We yu waahn?
8. Kom bak ya.
9. Luk ya?
10. Luk de?
11. Mi gal fren.
12. A fi mi sitn.
13. Im naasti op imself.
14. Wat a wie di gal priti!
15. Gi mi som a dat?
16. Mek wi go uova de.
17. A we dat?

18. Si im de!
19. Si dem de!
20. A we shi de?
21. Luk pan dis!
22. Bring mi a jringks
23. No bada mi.
24. Lef mi!
25. Di fuud kyan nyaam.
26. Kude!
27. Beg yu paas.
28. Waak gud.
29. Psst!!
30. Ton de so.

THE KEY

1. What's happening? How are you?
2. What are you doing?
3. What are you doing here?
4. Where are you going?
5. Where do you live?
6. Why did you call me?
7. What do you want?
8. Come back here.
9. Look here.
10. Look there.
11. My girlfriend.
12. It is mine/It belongs to me.
13. He/she is dirty.
14. The girl is beautiful.
15. Give me some of what you have?
16. Let us go over there.
17. What is that?
18. There he/she is.
19. There they are.
20. Where is she?
21. Look at this?
22. Beg you a drink?
23. Stop provoking me!

24. Leave me alone!
25. The food taste good!
26. Look at that!
27. Excuse me!
28. Take care of yourself.
29. Come here?
30. Go in that direction.

DIEZ A DI WIIK DEM

Sunday	Sonde
Monday	Monde
Tuesday	Chuuzde
Wednesday	Wenzde
Thursday	Torzde
Friday	Fraide
Saturday	Satde/Satide

MONT A DI IIR

January	Janiweri
February	Febiweri
March	Maach
April	Iepril

May	Mie
June	Juun
July	Julai
August	Aagos
September	Septemba
October	Aktuoba
November	Novemba
December	Disemba

BIBLIOGRAPHY

The Bible Society of the West Indies (2012), Di Jamiekan Nyuu Testiment, ISBN 978-0-564-02064-5.

Printed in Great Britain
by Amazon

?320421R00061